Handbook of Ballet

Editor

Masako Gillette

Scribbles

Year of Publication 2018

ISBN : 9789352979752

Book Published by

Scribbles

(An Imprint of Alpha Editions)

email - alphaedis@gmail.com

Produced by: PediaPress GmbH
Limburg an der Lahn
Germany
http://pediapress.com/

Contents

An Introduction

Ballet

<indicator name="pp-autoreview"> ☿ </indicator>

Ballet /ˈbæleɪ/ (French: [balɛ]) is a type of performance dance that originated during the Italian Renaissance in the 15th century and later developed into a concert dance form in France and Russia. It has since become a widespread, highly technical form of dance with its own vocabulary based on French terminology. It has been globally influential and has defined the foundational techniques used in many other dance genres and cultures. Ballet has been taught in various schools around the world, which have historically incorporated their own cultures and as a result, the art has evolved in a number of distinct ways. See glossary of ballet.

A *ballet*, a work, consists of the choreography and music for a ballet production. Ballets are choreographed and performed by trained ballet dancers. Traditional classical ballets are usually performed with classical music accompaniment and use elaborate costumes and staging, whereas modern ballets, such as the neoclassical works of American choreographer George Balanchine, often are performed in simple costumes (e.g., leotards and tights) and without the use of elaborate sets or scenery.

Etymology

Ballet is a French word which had its origin in Italian *balletto*, a diminutive of *ballo* (dance) which comes from Latin *ballo, ballare*, meaning "to dance", which in turn comes from the Greek "βαλλίζω" (*ballizo*), "to dance, to jump about". The word came into English usage from the French around 1630.

Figure 1: *Classical bell tutus in The Dance Class by Degas, 1874*

History

Ballet originated in the Italian Renaissance courts of the 15th and 16th centuries. Under Catherine de' Medici's influence as Queen, it spread to France, where it developed even further. The dancers in these early court ballets were mostly noble amateurs. Ornamented costumes were meant to impress viewers, but they restricted performers' freedom of movement.

The ballets were performed in large chambers with viewers on three sides. The implementation of the proscenium arch from 1618 on distanced performers from audience members, who could then better view and appreciate the technical feats of the professional dancers in the productions.Wikipedia:Citation needed

French court ballet reached its height under the reign of King Louis XIV. Louis founded the Académie Royale de Danse (Royal Dance Academy) in 1661 to establish standards and certify dance instructors. In 1672, Louis XIV made Jean-Baptiste Lully the director of the Académie Royale de Musique (Paris Opera) from which the first professional ballet company, the Paris Opera Ballet, arose. Pierre Beauchamp served as Lully's ballet-master. Together their partnership would drastically influence the development of ballet, as evidenced by the credit given to them for the creation of the five major positions of the

Figure 2: *Louis XIV as Apollo in the Ballet Royal de la Nuit (1653)*

feet. By 1681, the first "ballerinas" took the stage following years of training at the Académie.

Ballet started to decline in France after 1830, but it continued to develop in Denmark, Italy, and Russia. The arrival in Europe of the Ballets Russes led by Sergei Diaghilev on the eve of the First World War revived interest in the ballet and started the modern era.

In the 20th century, ballet had a wide influence on other dance genres, Also in the twentieth century, ballet took a turn dividing it from classical ballet to the introduction of modern dance, leading to modernist movements in several countries.

Famous dancers of the 20th century include Anna Pavlova, Galina Ulanova, Rudolf Nureyev, Maya Plisetskaya, Margot Fonteyn, Rosella Hightower, Maria Tall Chief, Erik Bruhn, Mikhail Baryshnikov, Suzanne Farrell, Gelsey Kirkland, Natalia Makarova, and Arthur Mitchell.

Figure 3: *Marie Sallé, classical ballet dancer*

Styles

Stylistic variations and subgenres have evolved over time. Early, classical variations are primarily associated with geographic origin. Examples of this are Russian ballet, French ballet, and Italian ballet. Later variations, such as contemporary ballet and neoclassical ballet, incorporate both classical ballet and non-traditional technique and movement. Perhaps the most widely known and performed ballet style is late Romantic ballet (or Ballet blanc).

Classical ballet

Classical ballet is based on traditional ballet technique and vocabulary. Different styles have emerged in different countries, such as French ballet, Italian ballet, English ballet, and Russian ballet. Several of the classical ballet styles are associated with specific training methods, typically named after their creators (see below). The Royal Academy of Dance method is a ballet technique and training system that was founded by a diverse group of ballet dancers. They merged their respective dance methods (Italian, French, Danish and Russian) to create a new style of ballet that is unique to the organization and is recognized internationally as the English style of ballet. Some examples of classical ballet productions are: *Swan Lake and the Nutcracker.*

Figure 4: *The Valse des cygnes from Act II of the Ivanov/Petipa edition of Swan Lake*

Romantic ballet

Romantic ballet was an artistic movement of classical ballet and several productions remain in the classical repertoire today. The Romantic era was marked by the emergence of pointe work, the dominance of female dancers, and longer, flowy tutus that attempt to exemplify softness and a delicate aura. This movement occurred during the early to mid 19th century (the Romantic era) and featured themes that emphasized intense emotion as a source of aesthetic experience. The plots of many romantic ballets revolved around spirit women (sylphs, wilis, and ghosts) who enslaved the hearts and senses of mortal men. The 1827 ballet *La Sylphide* is widely considered to be the first, and the 1870 ballet *Coppélia* is considered to be the last. Famous ballet dancers of the Romantic era include Marie Taglioni, Fanny Elssler, and Jules Perrot. Jules Perrot is also known for his choreography, especially that of Giselle, often considered to be the most widely celebrated romantic ballet.

Neoclassical ballet

Neoclassical ballet is usually abstract, with no clear plot, costumes or scenery. Music choice can be diverse and will often include music that is also neoclassical (e.g. Stravinsky, Roussel). Tim Scholl, author of *From Petipa to Balanchine*, considers George Balanchine's *Apollo* in 1928 to be the first neoclassical

Figure 5: *Carlotta Grisi, the original Giselle, 1841, wearing the romantic tutu*

ballet. *Apollo* represented a return to form in response to Sergei Diaghilev's abstract ballets. Balanchine worked with modern dance choreographer Martha Graham, and brought modern dancers into his company such as Paul Taylor, who in 1959 performed in Balanchine's *Episodes*.

While Balanchine is widely considered the face of neoclassical ballet, there were others who made significant contributions. Frederick Ashton's *Symphonic Variations* (1946) is a seminal work for the choreographer. Set to César Franck's score of the same title, it is a pure-dance interpretation of the score.

Another form, Modern Ballet, also emerged as an offshoot of neoclassicism. Among the innovators in this form were Glen Tetley, Robert Joffrey and Gerald Arpino. While difficult to parse modern ballet from neoclassicism, the work of these choreographers favored a greater athleticism that departed from the delicacy of ballet. The physicality was more daring, with mood, subject matter and music more intense. An example of this would be Joffrey's *Astarte* (1967), which featured a rock score and sexual overtones in the choreography.

Figure 6: *A contemporary ballet leap performed with modern, non-classical form*

Contemporary ballet

This ballet style is often performed barefoot. Contemporary ballets may include mime and acting, and are usually set to music (typically orchestral but occasionally vocal). It can be difficult to differentiate this form from neoclassical or modern ballet. Contemporary ballet is also close to contemporary dance, because many contemporary ballet concepts come from the ideas and innovations of 20th-century modern dance, including floor work and turn-in of the legs. The main distinction is that ballet technique is essential to perform a contemporary ballet.

George Balanchine is considered to have been a pioneer of contemporary ballet. Another early contemporary ballet choreographer, Twyla Tharp, choreographed *Push Comes To Shove* for the American Ballet Theatre in 1976, and in 1986 created *In The Upper Room* for her own company. Both of these pieces were considered innovative for their melding of distinctly modern movements with the use of pointe shoes and classically trained dancers.

Today there are many contemporary ballet companies and choreographers. These include Alonzo King and his company LINES Ballet; Matthew Bourne and his company New Adventures; Complexions Contemporary Ballet; Nacho Duato and his Compañia Nacional de Danza; William Forsythe and The

Forsythe Company; and Jiří Kylián of the Nederlands Dans Theater. Traditionally "classical" companies, such as the Mariinsky (Kirov) Ballet and the Paris Opera Ballet, also regularly perform contemporary works.

The term *ballet* has evolved to include all forms associated with it. Someone training as a ballet dancer will now be expected to perform neoclassical, modern and contemporary work. A ballet dancer is expected to be able to be stately and regal for classical work, free and lyrical in neoclassical work, and unassuming, harsh or pedestrian for modern and contemporary work. In addition, there are several modern varieties of dance that fuse classical ballet technique with contemporary dance, such as Hiplet, that require dancers to be practised in non-Western dance styles.

Technical methods of ballet instruction

There are six widely used, internationally recognized methods to teach or study ballet. These methods are the French School, the Vaganova Method, the Cecchetti Method, the Bournonville method, the Royal Academy of Dance method (English style), and the Balanchine method (American style). Many more schools of technique exist in various countries.

Figure 7: *Agrippina Vaganova, "Esmeralda" 1910*

French method

The French method is the basis of all ballet training. When Louis XIV created the Académie Royale de Danse in 1661, he helped to create the codified technique still used today by those in the profession, regardless of what method of training they adhere to. The French school was particularly revitalized under Rudolf Nureyev, in the 1980s. His influence revitalized and renewed appreciation for this style, and has drastically shaped ballet as a whole. In fact, the French school is now sometimes referred to as Nureyev school. The French method is often characterized by technical precision, fluidity and gracefulness, and elegant, clean lines. For this style, fast footwork is often utilized in order to give the impression that the performers are drifting lightly across the stage. Two important trademarks of this technique are the specific way in which the port de bras and the épaulement are performed, more rounded than when dancing in a Russian style, but not as rounded as the Danish style.

Vaganova method

The Vaganova method is a style of ballet training that emerged from Russian ballet, created by Agrippina Vaganova. After retiring from dance in 1916, Vaganova turned to teaching at the Leningrad Choreographic School in 1921. Her training method is now internationally recognized and revered and her

Figure 8: *Enrico Cecchetti with Anna Pavlova*

book, *The Fundamentals of Classical Dance*(1934), is a classic reference. This method is marked by the fusion of the classical French style, specifically elements from the Romantic era, with the athleticism of the Italian method, and the soulful passion of Russian ballet. She developed an extremely precise method of instruction in her book *Basic Principles of Russian Classical dance* (1948). This includes outlining when to teach technical components to students in their ballet careers, for how long to focus on it, and the right amount of focus at each stage of the student's career. These textbooks continue to be extremely important to the instruction of ballet today.

The method emphasizes development of strength, flexibility, and endurance for the proper performance of ballet. She espoused the belief that equal importance should be placed on the arms and legs while performing ballet, as this will bring harmony and greater expression to the body as a whole.

Cecchetti method

Developed by Enrico Cecchetti (1850-1928), this method is one known internationally for its intense reliance of the understanding of anatomy as it relates to classical ballet. The goal of this method is to instill important characteristics for the performance of ballet into students so that they do not need to rely on

Figure 9: *August Bournonville*

imitations of teachers. Important components for this method is the emphasis of balance, elevations, ballon, poise, and strength.

This method espouses the importance of recognizing that all parts of the body move together to create beautiful, graceful lines, and as such cautions against thinking of ballet in terms of the arms, legs, and neck and torso as separate parts. This method is well known for eight port de bras that are utilized.

Bournonville method

The Bournonville method is a Danish method first devised by August Bournonville. Bournonville was heavily influenced by the early French ballet method due to his training with his father, Antoine Bournonville and other important French ballet masters. This method has many style differences that differentiate it from other ballet methods taught today. A key component is the use of diagonal épaulements, with the upper body turning towards the working foot typically. This method also incorporates very basic use of arms, pirouettes from a low developpe position into seconde, and use of fifth position bras en bas for the beginning and end of movements.

The Bournonville method produces dancers who have beautiful *ballon* ("the illusion of imponderable lightness").

Figure 10: *Young girls competing at the Royal Academy of Dancing (London) exams held in Brisbane and Toowoomba, 1938*

The Royal Academy of Dance method (RAD)

The Royal Academy of Dance method, also referred to as the English style of ballet, was established in 1920 by Genee, Karsavina, Bedells, E Espinosa, and Richardson. The goal of this method is to promote academic training in classical ballet throughout Great Britain. This style also spread to the United States, and is widely utilized still today. There are specific grade levels which a student must move through in order to complete training in this method. The key principle behind this method of instruction is that basic ballet technique must be taught at a slow pace, with difficulty progression often much slower than the rest of the methods. The idea behind this is if a student is to put in a large amount of effort into perfecting the basic steps, the technique learned in these steps allow a student to utilize harder ones at a much easier rate.

Balanchine method

Developed by George Balanchine at the New York City Ballet. His method draws heavily on his own training as a dancer in Russia. The technique is known for extreme speed throughout routines, emphasis on lines, and deep pliés. Perhaps one of the most well known differences of this style is the unorthodox positioning of the body. Dancers of this style often have flexed hands

Figure 11: *Suzanne Farrell and George Balanchine danc-*
ing in a segment of "Don Quixote" at New York State Theater

and even feet, and are placed in off-balance positions. Important ballet studios teaching this method are the Miami City Ballet, Ballet Chicago Studio company, and the School of American Ballet in New York.

Costumes

Ballet costumes play an important role in the ballet community. They are often the only survival of a production, representing a living imaginary picture of the scene.

Renaissance and Baroque

The roots of ballet go back to the Renaissance in France and Italy when court wear was the beginning of ballet costumes. Ballet costumes have been around since the early fifteenth century. Cotton and silk were mixed with flax, woven into semitransparent gauze to create exquisite ballet costumes.

Figure 12: *Anna Pavlova (prima ballerina); Early materials for
ballet costumes were heavy, hindering the dancer's movements*

Seventeenth Century

During the seventeenth century, different types of fabrics and designs were
used to make costumes more spectacular and eye catching. Court dress still
remained for women during this century. Silks, satins and fabrics embroidered
with real gold and precious stones increased the level of spectacular decoration
associated with ballet costumes. Women's costumes also consisted of heavy
garments and knee-long skirts which made it difficult for them to create much
movement and gesture.

Eighteenth Century

During the eighteenth century, stage costumes were still very similar to court
wear but progressed over time, mostly due to the French dancer and ballet-
master Jean-Georges Noverre (1727 - 1810) whose proposals to modernize
ballet are contained in his revolutionary *Lettres sur la danse et les ballets*
(1760). Noverre's book altered the emphasis in a production away from the
costumes towards the physical movements and emotions of the dancers.

Figure 13: *Olga Spessiva; Swan Lake Costume in the 20th century*

European ballet was centered in the Paris Opera. During this era, skirts were raised a few inches off the ground. Flowers, flounces, ribbons, and lace emphasized this opulent feminine style, as soft pastel tones in citron, peach, pink and pistachio dominated the color range.

Nineteenth Century

During the early nineteenth century, close-fitting body costumes, floral crowns, corsages and jewels were used. Ideals of Romanticism were reflected through female movements. Costumes became much tighter as corsets started to come into use, to show off the curves on a ballerina. Jewels and bedazzled costumes became much more popular.

Twentieth Century

During the twentieth century, ballet costumes transitioned back to the influence of Russian ballet. Ballerina skirts became knee-length tutus, later on in order to show off their precise pointe work. Colors used on stage costumes also became much more vibrant. Designers used colors such as red, orange, yellow, etc. to create visual expression when ballet dancers perform on stage.

Further reading

- Anderson, Jack (1992). *Ballet & Modern Dance: A Concise History* (2nd ed.). Princeton, NJ: Princeton Book Company, Publishers. ISBN 0-87127-172-9.<templatestyles src="Module:Citation/CS1/styles.css"></templatestyles>
- Au, Susan (2002). *Ballet & Modern Dance* (2nd ed.). London: Thames & Hudson world of art. ISBN 0-500-20352-0.<templatestyles src="Module:Citation/CS1/styles.css"></templatestyles>
- Bland, Alexander (1976). *A History of Ballet and Dance in the Western World*. New York: Praeger Publishers. ISBN 0-275-53740-4.<templatestyles src="Module:Citation/CS1/styles.css"></templatestyles>
- Darius, Adam (2007). *Arabesques Through Time*. Harlequinade Books, Helsinki. <templatestyles src="Module:Citation/CS1/styles.css" />ISBN 951-98232-4-7
- Gordon, Suzanne (1984). *Off Balance: The Real World of Ballet*. McGraw-Hill. ISBN 0-07-023770-0.<templatestyles src="Module:Citation/CS1/styles.css"></templatestyles>
- Kant, Marion (2007). *Cambridge Companion to Ballet*. Cambridge Companions to Music (1st ed.). Cambridge,UK: Cambridge University Press, Publishers. ISBN 978-0-521-53986-9.<templatestyles src="Module:Citation/CS1/styles.css"></templatestyles>
- Kirstein, Lincoln; Stuart, Muriel (1952). *The Classic Ballet*. New York: Alfred A Knopf.<templatestyles src="Module:Citation/CS1/styles.css"></templatestyles>
- Lee, Carol (2002). *Ballet In Western Culture: A History of its Origins and Evolution*. New York: Routledge. ISBN 0-415-94256-X.<templatestyles src="Module:Citation/CS1/styles.css"></templatestyles>

External links

Wikimedia Commons has media related to *Ballet*.

シ か ゃ | Look up *ballet* in Wiktionary, the free dictionary.
λ ル ぃ
末 維 ⑰

- ⑩ Chisholm, Hugh, ed. (1911). "Ballet". *Encyclopædia Britannica* (11th ed.). Cambridge University Press.<templatestyles src="Module:Citation/CS1/styles.css"></templatestyles>

History

Timeline of ballet

A timeline of the history of ballet:

- 14th century
  - Medieval dance
- 15th century
- 16th century
  - Renaissance dance
  - Ballets de cour
  - Intermedio - Italian court spectaculars with dance
  - *Ballet Comique de la Reine* - sometimes called the "first ballet"
- 17th century
  - French ballet
  - Comédie-ballet
  - English country dance
- 18th century
  - Baroque dance
  - Opéra-ballet
  - Ballet d'action
- 19th century
  - Classical ballet (Russian ballet, Italian ballet)
  - Pre-romantic ballet
  - Romantic ballet
- 20th century
  - Modern ballet
  - Neoclassical ballet
  - Postmodern dance
  - Concert dance
  - Contemporary ballet
  - Post-structuralist ballet

Figure 14: *Engraving of the first scene of the Ballet Comique de la Reine, 1581.*

History of ballet

Ballet is a formalized form of dance with its origins in the Italian Renaissance courts of 15th and 16th centuries. Ballet spread from Italy to France with the help of Catherine de' Medici, where ballet developed even further under her aristocratic influence. An early example of Catherine's development of ballet is through 'Le Paradis d' Amour', a piece of work presented at her daughter's wedding, Marguerite de Valois to Henry of Navarre. Aristocratic money was responsible for the initial stages of development in 'court ballet', as it was royal money that dictated the ideas, literature and music used in ballets that were created to primarily entertain the aristocrats of the time. The first formal 'court ballet' ever recognized was staged in 1573, 'Ballet des Polonais'. In true form of royal entertainment, 'Ballet des Polonais' was commissioned by Catherine de' Medici to honor the Polish ambassadors who were visiting Paris upon the accession of Henry of Anjou to the throne of Poland. In 1581, Catherine de' Medici commissioned another court ballet, *Ballet Comique de la Reine*, however it was her compatriot, Balthasar de Beaujoyeulx, who organized the ballet. Catherine de' Medici and Balthasar de Beaujoyeulx were responsible for presenting the first court ballet ever to apply the principles of Baif's Academie, by integrating poetry, dance, music and set design to convey a unified dramatic

Figure 15: *A publicity photo for the premiere of Tchaikovsky's ballet The Sleeping Beauty (1890).*

storyline. Moreover, the early organization and development of 'court ballet' was funded by, influenced by and produced by the aristocrats of the time, fulfilling both their personal entertainment and political propaganda needs.

In the late 17th century Louis XIV founded the Académie Royale de Musique (the Paris Opera) within which emerged the first professional theatrical ballet company, the Paris Opera Ballet. The predominance of French in the vocabulary of ballet reflects this history. Theatrical ballet soon became an independent form of art, although still frequently maintaining a close association with opera, and spread from the heart of Europe to other nations. The Royal Danish Ballet and the Imperial Ballet of the Russian Empire were founded in the 1740s and began to flourish, especially after about 1850. In 1907 the Russian ballet in turn moved back to France, where the Ballets Russes of Sergei Diaghilev and its successors were particularly influential. Soon ballet spread around the world with the formation of new companies, including London's The Royal Ballet (1931), the San Francisco Ballet (1933), American Ballet Theatre (1937), The Royal Winnipeg Ballet (1939), The Australian Ballet (1940), the New York City Ballet (1948), the National Ballet of Canada (1951), and the National Ballet Academy and Trust of India (2002).[1]

In the 20th century styles of ballet continued to develop and strongly influence broader concert dance, for example, in the United States choreographer George Balanchine developed what is now known as neoclassical ballet, subsequent

Figure 16: *Engraving of the second scene of the Ballet Comique de la Reine, staged in Paris in 1581 for the French court.*

developments have included contemporary ballet and post-structural ballet, for example seen in the work of William Forsythe in Germany.

The etymology of the word "ballet" reflects its history. The word *ballet* comes from French and was borrowed into English around the 17th century. The French word in turn has its origins in Italian *balletto*, a diminutive of *ballo* (dance). *Ballet* ultimately traces back to Italian *ballare*, meaning *"to dance"*.[2]

Origins

Renaissance – Italy and France

Ballet originated in the Renaissance court as an outgrowth of court pageantry in Italy,[3] where aristocratic weddings were lavish celebrations. Tutus, ballet slippers and pointe work were not yet used. The choreography was adapted from court dance steps.[4] Performers dressed in fashions of the times. For women that meant formal gowns that covered their legs to the ankle. Early ballet was participatory, with the audience joining the dance towards the end.

Domenico da Piacenza (c. 1400–c. 1470) was one of the first dancing masters. Along with his students, Antonio Cornazzano and Guglielmo Ebreo da Pesaro, he was trained in dance and responsible for teaching nobles the art.

Da Piacenza left one work: *De arte saltandi et choreus ducendi* (On the art of dancing and conducting dances), which was put together by his students.[5] In 1489 Galeazzo, Duke of Milan, married Isabella of Aragon in Tortona. An elaborate dance entertainment was arranged for the celebrations by the Italian dance master Bergonzio di Botta. The dances were linked by a slim narrative concerning Jason and the Argonauts, and each corresponded to a different course for the dinner. Tristano Calco of Milan wrote about the event, and it was considered so impressive, that many similar spectacles were organized elsewhere.[6,7]

Ballet was further shaped by the French *ballet de cour*, which consisted of social dances performed by the nobility in tandem with music, speech, verse, song, pageant, decor and costume.[8] When Catherine de' Medici, an Italian aristocrat with an interest in the arts, married the French crown heir Henry II, she brought her enthusiasm for dance to France and provided financial support. Catherine's glittering entertainments supported the aims of court politics and usually were organized around mythological themes.[9] The first *ballet de cour* was the *Ballet de Polonais*. This Ballet was performed in 1573 on the occasion of the visit of the Polish Ambassador. It was choreographed by Balthasar de Beaaujoyeulx and featured an hour-long dance for sixteen women, each representing a French province. *Ballet Comique de la Reine* (1581), which was also choreographed and directed by Balthasar de Beaujoyeulx, was commissioned by Louise of Lorraine, queen consort of King Henry III, son of Catherine, to celebrate the marriage of Henry's favorite the Duke de Joyeuse to Marguerite de Lorraine, the sister of Queen Louise. The ballet lasted for more than five hours and was danced by twenty four dancers: twelve naiades and twelve pages.[10,11]

In the same year, the publication of Fabritio Caroso's *Il Ballarino*, a technical manual on court dancing, both performance and social, helped to establish Italy as a centre of technical ballet development.[12]

17th century – France and Court Dance

Ballet developed as a performance-focused art form in France during the reign of Louis XIV, who was passionate about dance.[13] Pierre Beauchamp, the man who codified the five basic positions of the feet in ballet, was the king's personal dance teacher and favorite partner in *ballet de cour* in the 1650s.[14] In 1661 Louis XIV, who was determined to reverse a decline in dance standards that began in the 17th century, established the Académie Royale de Danse. Beauchamp was appointed *Intendant des ballets du roi* and in 1680 became the director of the dance academy, a position he held until 1687.

Figure 17: *Louis XIV in Lully's Ballet Royal de la Nuit (1653).*

Jean-Baptiste Lully, an Italian violinist, dancer, choreographer, and composer, who joined the court of Louis XIV in 1652,[15] played a significant role in establishing the general direction ballet would follow for the next century. Supported and admired by King Louis XIV, Lully often cast the king in his ballets. The title of *Sun King* for the French monarch, originated in Louis XIV's role in Lully's *Ballet de la Nuit* (1653). The fourteen-year-old Louis XIV danced five roles in this 12-hour ballet.[16] This Ballet was lavish and featured a scene where a set piece of a house was burned down, included witches, werewolves, gypsies, shepherds, thieves, and the goddesses Venus and Diana. Lully's main contribution to ballet were his nuanced compositions. His understanding of movement and dance allowed him to compose specifically for ballet, with musical phrasings that complemented physical movements.[17] Lully also collaborated with the French playwright Molière. Together, they took an Italian theatre style, the *commedia dell'arte*, and adapted it into their work for a French audience, creating the *comédie-ballet*. Among their greatest productions, with Beauchamp as the choreographer, was *Le Bourgeois Gentilhomme* (1670).[18]

In 1669 Louis XIV founded the Académie d'Opéra with Pierre Perrin as director.[19] Louix XIV retired in 1670, largely because of excessive weight gain. Earlier, in 1661 he had founded a school, the *Adacemie Royale de danse*. Beauchamp was the first ballet-master of the Opéra and created the dances

Figure 18: *The Royal Ballet of the Dowager of Bilbao's Grand Ball, 1626.*

for the new company's first production *Pomone* with music by Robert Cambert. Later, after Perrin went bankrupt, the king reestablished the Opéra as the Académie royale de Musique and made Lully the director. Beauchamp was one of the principal choreographers. In this position Lully, with his librettist Philippe Quinault, created a new genre, the *tragédie en musique*, each act of which featured a *divertissement* that was a miniature ballet scene. With almost all his important creations Jean-Baptiste Lully brought together music and drama with Italian and French dance elements. His work created a legacy which would define the future of ballet.

Popularity throughout Europe

France's court was in some ways the leading source of fashionable culture for many other royal courts in Europe. Styles of entertainment were imitated, including the royal ballets. Courts in Spain, Portugal, Poland, Germany, and elsewhere all became audiences and participants in ballets. In addition to France, Italy became an important influence on the art form, predominantly Venice.

Professional ballet troupes began to organize and tour Europe, performing for aristocratic audiences. In Poland, King Władysław IV Vasa (1633–1648) hosted Italian opera productions, which included ballet performers in some scenes. The famous European ballet-masters who worked for the Polish court include Louis de Poitiers, Charles Duparc, Jean Favier, Antoine Pitrot, Antonio Sacco and Francesco Caselli.

18th century

France and development as an art form

The 18th century was a period of advance in the technical standards of ballet and the period when ballet became a serious dramatic art form on par with the opera. Central to this advance was the seminal work of Jean-Georges Noverre, *Lettres sur la danse et les ballets* (1760), which focused on developing the ballet d'action, in which the movements of the dancers are designed to express character and assist in the narrative. Noverre believed that: ballet should be technical but also move the audience emotionally, plots need to be unified, the scenery and music need to support the plot and be unified within the story, and that pantomime needs to be simple and understandable.[20]

Reforms were made in ballet composition by composers such as Christoph Willibald Gluck. Finally, ballet was divided into three formal techniques *sérieux*, *demi-caractère* and *comique*. Ballet also began to be featured in operas as interludes called divertissements.

Outside France

Venice continued to be a centre of dance in Europe, particularly during the Venice Carnival, when dancers and visitors from across the continent would travel to the city for a lively cultural exchange. The city's Teatro San Benedetto became a famous landmark largely due to the ballets performed there. Italian ballet techniques remained the dominant influence in much of southern and eastern Europe until Russian techniques supplanted them in the early 20th century.

Ballet performances spread to Eastern Europe during the 18th century, into areas such as Hungary, where they were held in private theatres at aristocratic castles. Professional companies were established that performed throughout Hungary and also toured abroad. The Budapest National Theatre increasingly serving a role as a home for the dancers.

Some of the leading dancers of the time who performed throughout Europe were Louis Dupré, Charles Le Picque with Anna Binetti, Gaetano Vestris, and Jean-Georges Noverre.

Figure 19: *Polish ballet performers at the 1827 Venice Carnival. The dancer on the left is performing "en travestie" as a woman taking the man's role.*

19th century

The ballerina became the most popular dance performer in Europe in the first half of the 19th century, gradually turning the spotlight away from the male dancer. In many performances, ballet heroes were played by a woman, like the Principal Boy in pantomime.

The professionalism of ballet companies became a focus for a new generation of ballet masters and dancers. Vienna was an important source of influential ballet coaches. The first ballet master of Hungary's National Theatre and Royal Opera was the Vienna-born Frigyes Campilli, who worked in Budapest for 40 years.

The 19th century was a period of great social change, which was reflected in ballet by a shift away from the aristocratic sensibilities that had dominated earlier periods through romantic ballet. Ballerinas such as Geneviève Gosselin, Marie Taglioni and Fanny Elssler experimented with new techniques such as pointework that gave the ballerina prominence as the ideal stage figure. Taglioni was known as the "Christian Dancer," as her image was light and pure (associated with her role as the sylph in La Sylphide). She was trained primarily by her father, Filipo Taglioni. In 1834, Fanny Elssler arrived at the Paris Opera and became known as the "Pagan Dancer," because of the fiery

Figure 20: *Marie Taglioni as Flore in Charles Didelot's ballet Flore et Zéphire (ca. 1831). She was a pioneer of pointework.*

qualities of the *Cachucha* dance that made her famous. Professional librettists began crafting the stories in ballets. Teachers like Carlo Blasis codified ballet technique in the basic form that is still used today. The ballet boxed toe shoe was invented to support pointe work.

Romantic movement

The Romantic movement in art, literature, and theatre was a reaction against formal constraints and the mechanics of industrialization.[22] The zeitgeist led choreographers to compose romantic ballets that appeared light, airy and free that would act as a contrast to the spread of reductionist science through many aspects of daily life that had, in the words of Poe, "driven the hamadryad from the woods". These "unreal" ballets portrayed women as fragile unearthly beings, ethereal creatures who could be lifted effortlessly and almost seemed to float in the air. Ballerinas began to wear costumes with pastel, flowing skirts that bared the shins. The stories revolved around uncanny, folkloric spirits. An example of one such romantic ballet is *La Sylphide*, one of the oldest romantic ballets still performed today.

One strain of the Romantic movement was a new exploration of folklore and traditional ethnic culture. This influence was seen in the emergence of European folk dance and western portrayals of African, Asian, and Middle East

Figure 21: *Mikhail Mordkin as Prince Siegfried and Adelaide Giuri as Odette with students as the little swans in the Moscow Imperial Bolshoi Theatre's production of the Petipa/Ivanov/Tchaikovsky Swan Lake. 1901*

peoples on European stages. In ballets from this period, non-European characters were often created as villains or as silly divertisements to fit the orientalist western understanding of the world. The National Opera of Ukraine, a performing arts theatre with a resident opera company, was established in Kiev in 1867. It also included a small resident troupe of ballet dancers, who would perform mainly folk-style dancing during opera productions. By 1893, this grew to a troupe large enough to stage large ballets. Folk dancing and ballets with Ukrainian stories were among the early productions.

Many leading European professional ballet companies that survive today were established at new theatres in Europe's capital cities during the mid- to late-19th century, including the Kiev Ballet, the Hungarian National Ballet, the National Theatre Ballet (Prague) and the Vienna State Ballet (formerly the Vienna State Opera Ballet). These theatres usually combined large opera, drama and ballet companies under the same roof. Composers, dramatists, and choreographers were then able to create works that took advantage of the ability to collaborate among these performance troupes.

Russia

While France was instrumental in early ballet, other countries and cultures soon adopted the art form, most notably Russia. Russia has a recognized tradition of ballet, and Russian ballet has had great importance in its country throughout history. After 1850, ballet began to wane in Paris, but it flourished in Denmark and Russia thanks to masters such as August Bournonville, Jules Perrot, Arthur Saint-Léon, Enrico Cecchetti and Marius Petipa. In the late nineteenth century, orientalism was in vogue. Colonialism brought awareness of Asian and African cultures, but distorted with disinformation and fantasy. The East was often perceived as a faraway place where anything was possible, provided it was lavish, exotic and decadent. Petipa appealed to popular taste with *The Pharaoh's Daughter* (1862), and later *The Talisman* (1889), and *La Bayadère* (1877). Petipa is best remembered for his collaborations with Tchaikovsky. He used his music for his choreography of *The Nutcracker* (1892, though this is open to some debate among historians), *The Sleeping Beauty* (1890), and the definitive revival of *Swan Lake* (1895, with Lev Ivanov). These works were all drawn from European folklore.

The female dancers' classical tutu as it is recognized today began to appear at this time. It consisted of a short, stiff skirt supported by layers of crinoline or tulle that revealed the acrobatic legwork, combined with a wide gusset that served to preserve modesty.

Argentina

Ballet companies from Europe began lucrative tours of theatres in North, Central and South America during the mid-19th century. The prestigious Colon Theater in Buenos Aires, Argentina had hosted foreign ballet artists on its stage, with touring companies from Europe presenting full ballets as early as 1867. By the 1880s, the Colon Theater had its own professional ballet company. It would still be several decades before most countries outside of Europe could claim their own professional ballet companies, however.

20th century and modernism

Russia and the Ballets Russes

Sergei Diaghilev brought ballet full-circle back to Paris when he opened his company, Ballets Russes. It was made up of dancers from the Russian exile community in Paris after the Revolution.

Diaghilev and composer Igor Stravinsky merged their talents to bring Russian folklore to life in *The Firebird* and *Petrushka* choreographed by Fokine. Diaghilev's next choreographic commissions went to Nijinsky. His First ballet

Figure 22: *Anna Pavlova as a bacchante in Bacchanale by Mikhail Mordkin.*

was *L'apres-midi d'un Faune* (Afternoon of a Faun) to music by Debussy. It was notable for its two dimensional shapes and lack of ballet technique. It caused controversy by depicting the faun rubbing the scarf of one of the maidens on himself, in simulated masturbation. The most controversial work of the Ballets Russes however, was *The Rite of Spring*, choreographed by Nijinsky with music by Stravinsky. The ballet's modern music, pigeon toed stomping and theme of human sacrifice shocked audiences so much they rioted.

After the "golden age" of Petipa, Michel Fokine began his career in St. Petersburg but moved to Paris and worked with Diaghilev and the Ballets Russes.

Russian ballet continued development under Soviet rule. There was little talent left in the country after the Revolution, but it was enough to seed a new generation. After stagnation in the 1920s, by the mid-1930s that new generation of dancers and choreographers appeared on the scene. The technical perfection and precision of dance was promoted (and demanded) by Agrippina Vaganova, who had been taught by Petipa and Cecchetti and headed the Vaganova Ballet Academy, the school to prepare dancers for the Kirov Ballet in St. Petersburg/Leningrad.

Ballet was popular with the public. Both the Moscow-based Bolshoi and the St. Petersburg (then Leningrad)-based Kirov ballet companies were active. Ideological pressure forced the creation of many socialist realist pieces, most

Figure 23: *Vaslav Nijinsky in The Spectre of the Rose, 1911.*

of which made little impression on the public and were removed from the repertoire of both companies later.

Some pieces of that era, however, were remarkable. The *Romeo and Juliet* by Prokofiev and Lavrovsky is a masterpiece. The *Flames of Paris*, while it shows all the faults of socialist realist art, pioneered the active use of the corps de ballet in the performance and required stunning virtuosity. The ballet version of the Pushkin poem, *The Fountain of Bakhchisarai* with music from Boris Asafiev and choreography by Rostislav Zakharov was also a hit.

The well-known ballet *Cinderella*, for which Prokofiev provided the music, is also the product of the Soviet ballet. During the Soviet era, these pieces were mostly unknown outside the Soviet Union and later outside of the Eastern Bloc. However, after the collapse of the Soviet Union they received more recognition.

The 1999 North American premiere of *The Fountain of Bakhchisarai* by the Kirov Ballet in New York was an outstanding success, for example. The Soviet era of the Russian Ballet put a lot of emphasis on technique, virtuosity and strength. It demanded strength usually above the norm of contemporary Western dancers. When watching restored old footage, one can only marvel at the talent of their prima ballerinas such as Galina Ulanova, Natalya Dudinskaya and Maya Plisetskaya and choreographers such as Pyotr Gusev.

Figure 24: *The Dying Swan choreographed by Fokine, performed by three soloists (shown in order): 1. Anna Pavlova (7 seconds) 2. Yvette Chauvire (10 seconds) 3. Natalia Makarova (14 seconds).*

Russian companies, particularly after World War II engaged in multiple tours all over the world that revitalized ballet in the West.

Maiden Tower[21] written by Afrasiyab Badalbeyli is the first ballet in the Muslim East.[22,23]

United States of America

Following the move of the Ballets Russes to France, ballet began to have a broader influence, particularly in the United States of America.

From Paris, after disagreements with Diaghilev, Fokine went to Sweden and then the USA and settled in New York. Diaghilev believed that traditional ballet offered little more than prettiness and athletic display. For Fokine that was not enough. In addition to technical virtuosity he demanded drama, expression and historical authenticity. The choreographer must research the period and cultural context of the setting and reject the traditional tutu in favour of accurate period costuming.

Fokine choreographed *Sheherazade* and *Cleopatra*. He also reworked *Petrouchka* and *The Firebird*. One of his most famous works was *The Dying Swan*, performed by Anna Pavlova. Beyond her talents as a ballerina, Pavlova had the theatrical gifts to fulfill Fokine's vision of ballet as drama. Legend has it that Pavlova identified so much with the swan role that she requested her swan costume from her deathbed.

George Balanchine developed state-of-the-art technique in America by opening a school in Chicago and more importantly, in New York. He adapted ballet to the new media, movies and television.[24] A prolific worker, Balanchine rechoreographed classics such as *Swan Lake* and *Sleeping Beauty* as well as creating new ballets. He produced original interpretations of the dramas of William Shakespeare such as *Romeo and Juliet* and *A Midsummer Night's Dream*, and also of Franz Léhar's *The Merry Widow*.

In 1967, Balanchine's *Jewels* broke with the narrative tradition and dramatized a theme rather than a plot. This focus fits with the state-sponsored funding sources in the United States which sought to encourage "liberty and free-thinking" in contrast to narrative-driven dance, which was seen as to be connected too closely with socialism, especially Soviet communism. Today, partly thanks to Balanchine, ballet is one of the most well-preserved dances in the world.Wikipedia:Citation needed

Barbara Karinska was a Russian emigree and a skilled seamstress who collaborated with Balanchine to elevate the art of costume design from a secondary role to an integral part of a ballet performance. She introduced the bias cut and a simplified classic tutu that allowed the dancer more freedom of movement. With meticulous attention to detail, she decorated her tutus with beadwork, embroidery, crochet and appliqué.

Neoclassical ballet

George Balanchine is often considered to have been the first pioneer of what is now known as neoclassical ballet, a style of dance between classical ballet and today's contemporary ballet. Tim Scholl, author of *From Petipa to Balanchine*, considers Balanchine's *Apollo* (1928) to be the first neoclassical ballet. It represented a return to form in response to Serge Diaghilev's abstract ballets. *Apollo* and other works are still performed today, predominantly by the New York City Ballet. However, other companies are able to pay a fee for performance rights to George Balanchine's works.

Frederick Ashton is another prominent choreographer associated with the neoclassical style. Three of his works have become standard pieces in the international repertoire: *Sylvia* (1952), *Romeo and Juliet* (1956), and *Ondine* (1958), the last of which was created as a vehicle to showcase Margot Fonteyn.

Contemporary

One dancer who trained with Balanchine and absorbed much of this neoclassical style was Mikhail Baryshnikov. Following Baryshnikov's appointment as artistic director of American Ballet Theatre in 1980, he worked with various modern choreographers, most notably Twyla Tharp. Tharp choreographed *Push Comes To Shove* for ABT and Baryshnikov in 1976; in 1986

Figure 25: *Ballets Russes with Apollo (1928) choreographed by George Balanchine. Dancers are Alexandrova Danilova and Serge Lifar.*

Figure 26: *A 2010 performance of Irène Tassem-bédo's contemporary ballet piece Allah Garibou.*

she created *In The Upper Room* for her own company. Both these pieces were considered innovative for their use of distinctly modern movements melded with the use of pointe shoes and classically trained dancers—for their use of contemporary ballet.

Tharp also worked with the Joffrey Ballet company, founded in 1957 by Robert Joffrey. She choreographed *Deuce Coupe* for them in 1973, using pop music and a blend of modern and ballet techniques. The Joffrey Ballet continued to perform numerous contemporary pieces, many choreographed by co-founder Gerald Arpino.

Today there are many contemporary ballet companies and choreographers. These include Madrid Ballet; Royal Ballet of Flanders; Alonzo King and his company, Alonzo King LINES Ballet; Nacho Duato and Compañia Nacional de Danza; William Forsythe, who has worked extensively with the Frankfurt Ballet and today runs The Forsythe Company; and Jiří Kylián, formerly the artistic director of the Nederlands Dans Theater. Traditionally "classical" companies, such as the Kirov Ballet and the Paris Opera Ballet, also regularly perform contemporary works.

Development of ballet method

Several well-known ballet methods are named after their originators. For example, two prevailing systems from Russia are known as the Vaganova method after Agrippina Vaganova, and the Legat Method, after Nikolai Legat. The Cecchetti method was invented by Italian dancer Enrico Cecchetti (1850–1928), and the Bournonville method, which was invented by August Bournonville (1805–1879), is employed chiefly in Bournonville's own country of Denmark.

Further reading

- Anderson, Jack (1992). *Ballet & Modern Dance: A Concise History* (2nd ed.). Princeton, NJ: Princeton Book Company, Publishers. ISBN 0-87127-172-9.<templatestyles src="Module:Citation/CS1/styles.css"></templatestyles>
- Andre, Paul; Arkadyev, V. (1999) *Great History of Russian Ballet: Its Art & Choreography* (1999).
- Bland, Alexander (1976). *A History of Ballet and Dance in the Western World*. New York: Praeger Publishers. ISBN 0-275-53740-4.<templatestyles src="Module:Citation/CS1/styles.css"></templatestyles>

- Caddy, Davinia. (2012). *The Ballets Russes and Beyond: Music and Dance in Belle-Epoque Paris*. Cambridge: Cambridge University Press.
- Cohen, Selma Jeanne, founding editor (1998). *International Encyclopedia of Dance*. New York: Oxford University Press.<templatestyles src="Module:Citation/CS1/styles.css"></templatestyles>
- Cross, Samuel H. (1944) "The Russian Ballet Before Dyagilev." *Slavonic and East European Review. American Series* 3.4 (1944): 19-49. in JSTOR[25]
- Ezrahi, Christina. (2012) *Swans of the Kremlin: Ballet and Power in Soviet Russia* (University of Pittsburgh Press); examines the resilience of artistic creativity in a history of the Bolshoi and Marinsky/Kirov ballets
- Franko, Mark (1993). *Dance as Text: Ideologies of the Baroque Body*. Cambridge: Cambridge University Press.<templatestyles src="Module:Citation/CS1/styles.css"></templatestyles>
- Homans, Jennifer, (2010). *Apollo's Angels: A History of Ballet*. New York: Random House.
- Johnson, Alfred Edwin. (1913) *The Russian Ballet* (Houghton Mifflin) online[26]
- Kassing, Gayle. (2007). *History of dance : an interactive arts approach*. Champaign, IL: Human Kinetics.<templatestyles src="Module:Citation/CS1/styles.css"></templatestyles>
- Lee, Carol (2002). *Ballet In Western Culture: A History of its Origins and Evolution*. New York: Routledge. ISBN 0-415-94256-X.<templatestyles src="Module:Citation/CS1/styles.css"></templatestyles>
- Lifar, Serge. (1954). *A history of Russian ballet from its origins to the present day* (Hutchinson)
- McGowan, Margaret M. (1978). *L'art du ballet de cour en France, 1581–1643*. Paris: Centre National de la Recherche Scientifique.<templatestyles src="Module:Citation/CS1/styles.css"></templatestyles>
- Propert, Walter Archibald. (1972) *The Russian Ballet in Western Europe, 1909-1920*. B. Blom
- Roslavleva, Natalia. (1966). *Era of the Russian Ballet,* New York: E.P. Dutton & Co., Inc.
- Sadie, Stanley, ed. (1992). *The new Grove dictionary of opera* (4 volumes). London: Macmillan. ISBN 978-1-56159-228-9.<templatestyles src="Module:Citation/CS1/styles.css"></templatestyles>
- Surits̃, E. I͡A, and E. I꠸A꠸ Surit꠸s꠸. (1990) *Soviet Choreographers in the 1920s* (Duke Univ Press, 1990).
- Wiley, Roland John. (1990) *A century of Russian ballet: documents and accounts, 1810-1910* (Oxford University Press)

Styles

Classical ballet

Classical ballet is any of the traditional, formal styles of ballet that exclusively employ classical ballet technique. It is known for its aesthetics and rigorous technique (such as pointe work, turnout of the legs, and high extensions), its flowing, precise movements, and its ethereal qualities.

There are stylistic variations related to an area or origin, which are denoted by classifications such as Russian ballet, French ballet, British ballet and Italian ballet. For example, Russian ballet features high extensions and dynamic turns, whereas Italian ballet tends to be more grounded, with a focus on fast, intricate footwork. Many of the stylistic variations are associated with specific training methods that have been named after their originators. Despite these variations, the performance and vocabulary of classical ballet are largely consistent throughout the world.

History

Ballet originated in the Italian Renaissance courts and was brought to France by Catherine de' Medici in the 16th Century. During ballet's infancy, court ballets were performed by aristocratic amateurs rather than professional dancers. Most of ballet's early movements evolved from social court dances and prominently featured stage patterns rather than formal ballet technique.

In the 17th century, as ballet's popularity in France increased, ballet began to gradually transform into a professional art. It was no longer performed by amateurs, but instead ballet performances started to incorporate challenging acrobatic movements that could only be performed by highly skilled street entertainers. In response, the world's first ballet school, the Académie Royale de Danse, was established by King Louis XIV in 1661. The Academie's purpose was to improve the quality of dance training in France, and to invent a

Figure 27: *Painting of ballet dancers by Edgar Degas, 1872.*

technique or curriculum that could be used to transform ballet into a formal discipline. Shortly after the Academie was formed, in 1672, King Louis XIV established a performing company called the Academie Royal de Musique de Dance (today known as Paris Opera), and named Pierre Beauchamp the head dancing-master. While at the Academie Royal, Beauchamp revolutionized ballet technique by inventing the five positions (first, second, third, fourth and fifth) of ballet, which to this day remain the foundation of all formal classical ballet technique.

Technique

Ballet technique is the foundational principles of body movement and form used in ballet. A distinctive feature of ballet technique is *turnout;* which is the outward rotation of the legs and feet emanating from the hip. This was first introduced into ballet by King Louis XIV because he loved to show off the shiny buckles on his shoes when he performed his own dances. There are five fundamental positions of the feet in ballet, all performed with turnout and named numerically as *first* through *fifth* positions. When performing jumps and leaps, classical ballet dancers strive to exhibit *ballon*, the appearance of briefly floating in the air. *Pointe technique* is the part of ballet technique that concerns *pointe work*, in which a ballet dancer supports all body weight on the

Figure 28: *Marie Taglioni, a pioneer of pointe work.*

tips of fully extended feet on specially designed and handcrafted *pointe shoes*. In professional companies, the shoes are made to fit the dancers' feet perfectly.

Training

Students typically learn ballet terminology and the pronunciation, meaning, and precise body form and movement associated with each term. Emphasis is placed on developing flexibility and strengthening the legs, feet, and body core (the *center*, or abdominals) as a strong core is essential for turns and many other ballet movements. Dancers also learn to use their *spot* which teaches them to focus on something while turning so as not to become dizzy and lose their balance.

After learning basic ballet technique and developing sufficient strength and flexibility, female dancers begin to learn pointe technique and male and female dancers begin to learn partnering and more advanced jumps and turns. Depending on the teacher and training system, students may progress through various stages or levels of training as their skills advance.

Figure 29: *Ballerina dancing en pointe*

Ballet class attire

Female attire typically includes pink or flesh colored tights, a leotard, and sometimes a short wrap-skirt, or a skirted leotard. Males typically wear black or dark tights, a form-fitting white, or black, shirt or leotard worn under the tights, and a dance belt beneath the outer dancewear to provide support. In some cases, students may wear a unitard — a one-piece garment that combines tights and a leotard — to enhance the visibility of artistic lines.

All dancers wear soft ballet shoes (sometimes called *flats*). Typically, female dancers wear pink or beige shoes and men wear black or white shoes. Leg warmers are sometimes worn during the early part of a class to protect leg muscles until they become warm. Females are usually required to restrain their hair in a bun or some other hair style that exposes the neck that is not a ponytail. The customary attire and hair style are intended to promote freedom of movement and to reveal body form so that the teacher can evaluate dancers' alignment and technique. After warming up, advanced female students may wear pointe shoes whereas advanced male students continue to wear soft shoes. Pointe shoes are worn after the student is deemed strong enough in the ankles and can execute the routine to a high standard, usually around or after the age of 12, or after the dancers' feet have stopped developing, so as to protect the dancers' feet from injury common with premature wearing.

Methods

There are several standardized, widespread, classical ballet training systems, each designed to produce a unique aesthetic quality from its students. Some systems are named after their creators; these are typically called *methods* or *schools*. For example, two prevailing systems from Russia are the Vaganova method (created by Agrippina Vaganova) and the Legat Method (by Nikolai Legat). The Cecchetti method is named after Italian dancer Enrico Cecchetti. Another training system was developed by and named after August Bournonville; this is taught primarily in Denmark. The Royal Academy of Dance (RAD) method was not created by an individual, but by a group of notable ballet professionals. Despite their associations with geographically named ballet styles, many of these training methods are used worldwide. For example, the RAD teaching method is used in more than 70 countries.

American-style ballet (Balanchine) is not taught by means of a standardized, widespread training system. Similarly, French ballet has no standard training system; each of the major French-style ballet schools, such as the Paris Opera Ballet School, Conservatoire National Supérieur de Musique et de Danse, and Académie de Danse Classique Princesse Grace (Monaco) employs a unique training system.

Widely used ballet training systems

Ballet style	Training system	
	Name	Creator
Danish ballet	Bournonville method	August Bournonville
Italian ballet	Cecchetti method	Enrico Cecchetti
Russian ballet	Vaganova method	Agrippina Vaganova
	Legat Method	Nikolai Legat
English ballet	Royal Academy of Dance	Various
French ballet	None	
American ballet (Balanchine)	None	

Stage reference points

Some classical ballet training systems employ standardized layouts to define reference locations at the corners, and edges of stages, and dance studio rooms. In the latter case, there is no audience and a mirror typically spans the downstage wall of the room (e.g., points 1-2 of the Cecchetti layout).

<templatestyles src="Gallery/styles.css" />

Stage layouts used in ballet training systems

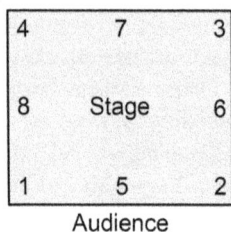

Audience

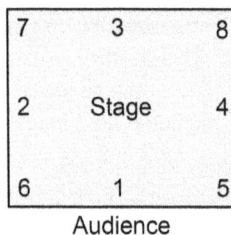

Audience

Cecchetti stage layout

RAD stage layout

Vaganova stage layout

External links

- "Beginner's Guide to Ballet"[27] (PDF). Archived from the original[28] (PDF) on 2008-04-05.<templatestyles src="Module:Citation/CS1/styles.css"></templatestyles> (3.47 MiB)

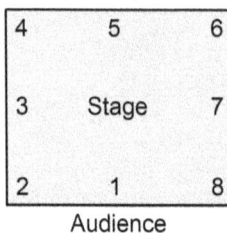

Audience

Sources

- Anderson, Jack (1992). *Ballet & Modern Dance: A Concise History* (2nd ed.). Princeton, NJ: Princeton Book Company, Publishers. ISBN 0-87127-172-9.<templatestyles src="Module:Citation/CS1/styles.css"></templatestyles>
- Bland, Alexander (1976). *A History of Ballet and Dance in the Western World.* New York: Praeger Publishers. ISBN 0-275-53740-4.<templatestyles src="Module:Citation/CS1/styles.css"></templatestyles>
- Chantrell, Glynnis, ed. (2002). *The Oxford Essential Dictionary of Word Histories.* New York: Berkley Books. ISBN 0-425-19098-6.<templatestyles src="Module:Citation/CS1/styles.css"></templatestyles>
- Kirstein, Lincoln; Stuart, Muriel (1952). *The Classic Ballet.* New York: Alfred A Knopf.<templatestyles src="Module:Citation/CS1/styles.css"></templatestyles>
- Lee, Carol (2002). *Ballet In Western Culture: A History of its Origins and Evolution.* New York: Routledge. ISBN 0-415-94256-X.<templatestyles src="Module:Citation/CS1/styles.css"></templatestyles>

Romantic ballet

The **Romantic ballet** is defined primarily by an era in ballet in which the ideas of Romanticism in art and literature influenced the creation of ballets. The era occurred during the early to mid 19th century primarily at the Théâtre de l'Académie Royale de Musique of the Paris Opera Ballet and Her Majesty's Theatre in London. It is typically considered to have begun with the 1827 début in Paris of the ballerina Marie Taglioni in the ballet *La Sylphide*, and to have reached its zenith with the premiere of the divertissement *Pas de Quatre* staged by the Ballet Master Jules Perrot in London in 1845. The Romantic ballet had no immediate end, but rather a slow decline. Arthur Saint-Léon's 1870 ballet *Coppélia* is considered to be the last work of the Romantic Ballet.

During this era, the development of pointework, although still at a fairly basic stage, profoundly affected people's perception of the ballerina. Many lithographs of the period show her virtually floating, poised only on the tip of a toe. This idea of weightlessness was capitalised on in ballets such as *La Sylphide* and *Giselle*, and the famous leap apparently attempted by Carlotta Grisi in *La Péri*.

Figure 30: *The Three Graces: embodiment of the Romantic ballet, ca. 1840. This lithograph by A. E. Chalon depicts three of the greatest ballerinas in three of the era's defining roles: (left to right) Marie Taglioni as the Sylph in Filippo Taglioni's 1832 ballet La Sylphide; Fanny Elssler as Florinda in the dance La Cachucha from Jean Coralli's 1836 ballet Le Diable boiteux; and Carlotta Grisi as Béatrix in the Grand pas de Diane chasseresse from Albert's 1842 ballet La Jolie Fille du Gand.*

Other features which distinguished Romantic ballet were the separate identity of the scenarist or author from the choreographer, and the use of specially written music as opposed to a *pastiche* typical of the ballet of the late 18th and early 19th centuries. The invention of gas lighting enabled gradual changes and enhanced the mysteriousness of many ballets with its softer gleam. Illusion became more diverse with wires and trap doors being widely used.

Cult of the ballerina

The Romantic era marked the rise of the ballerina as a central part of ballet, where previously men had dominated performances. There had always been admiration for superior dancers, but elevating ballerinas to the level of celebrity came into its own in the nineteenth century, especially as female performers became idealized and objectified. Marie Taglioni became the prototypical Romantic ballerina, praised highly for her lyricism. The movement style for Romantic ballerinas was characterized by soft, rounded arms and

Figure 31: *Lithograph by A. E. Chalon of Carlotta Grisi (left), Marie Taglioni (center), Lucille Grahn (right back), and Fanny Cerrito (right front) in the Perrot/Pugni Pas de Quatre, London, 1845. The premiere of the Pas de Quatre is considered to be the Romantic ballet at its zenith.*

a forward tilt in the upper body. This gave the woman a flowery, willowy look. Leg movements became more elaborate due to the new tutu length and rising standards of technical proficiency. Important Romantic ballerinas included Marie Taglioni, Carlotta Grisi, Lucille Grahn, Fanny Cerrito, Pauline Leroux and Fanny Elssler. The plots of many ballets were dominated by spirit women—sylphs, wilis, and ghosts, who enslaved the hearts and senses of mortal men and made it impossible for them to live happily in the real world.

While ballerinas became increasingly virtuosic, male dancers became scarce, particularly in Paris (although they were still common in other European areas, such as Denmark). This led to the rise of the female travesty dancer - a female dancer who played male roles. While travesty dancing had existed prior to the romantic period it was generally used in tableau and walk-on (marcheuse) parts. Now it became a high-status occupation, and a number of prima ballerinas made their names by dancing *en travestie*. Fanny Elssler and her sister both played travesty parts. The most well known travesty dancer was Eugénie Fiocre, who was the first dancer to play Frantz in *Coppélia*, as well as a number of ballerina roles.

Figure 32: *A romantic tutu*

Design and scenography

Romantic tutu

The costume for the Romantic ballerina was the romantic tutu. This was a full, white, multi-layered skirt made of tulle. The ballerina wore a white bodice with the tutu. In the second acts of Romantic ballets, representing the spiritual realm, the *corps de ballet* appeared on stage in Romantic tutus, giving rise to the term "white act" or ballet-blanc. The dancers wore pointe shoes to give the effect of floating. However, sometimes they decided to throw in extra sharp, sassy movements to portray the given concept or intent, often using high kicks and fast turns.

Special effects

Romantic ballet owed much to the new developments in theatre effects, particularly gas lighting. Candles had been previously used to light theatres, but gas lighting allowed for dimming effects and other subtleties. Combined with the effects of the Romantic tutu, ballerinas posing *en pointe*, and the use of wires to make dancers "fly," directors used gas lighting to create supernatural spectacles on stage.

Famous ballets

- *La Somnambule* (1827)
- *La Sylphide* (1832)
- *Le Diable boiteux*fr:Le Diable boiteux (ballet) (1836)
- *La Fille du Danube* (1836)
- *La Gipsy* (1839)
- *Le Diable amoureux* (1840)
- *Giselle* (1841)
- *La Jolie Fille de Gand* (1842)
- *La Péri* (1843)
- *Ondine* (1843)
- *La Vivandière or Markitenka* (1844)
- *La Esmeralda* (1844)
- *Éoline, ou La Dryade* (1845)
- *Le Diable à Quatre* (1845)
- *Pas de Quatre* (1845)
- *Catarina, or La Fille du Bandit* (1846)
- *Le Jugement de Paris* (1846)
- *Paquita* (1846)
- *La Fille de marbre* (1847)
- *Electra, ou La Pléiade perdue* (1849)
- *Le Violon du diable* (1849)
- *La Filleule des fées* (1849)
- *Les Métamorphoses* (1850)
- *Vert-Vert* (1851)
- *Le Corsaire* (1856)
- *Le Papillon* (1861)
- *Coppélia* (1870)

Notable choreographers

- Albert
- Jean Coralli
- Joseph Mazilier
- Jules Perrot
- Marius Petipa
- Arthur Saint-Léon
- Filippo Taglioni
- Paul Taglioni

Notable composers

- Adolphe Adam
- Cesare Pugni

Notable theatres

- Her Majesty's Theatre, London
- Théâtre de l'Académie Royale de Musique of the Paris Opera Ballet

Neoclassical ballet

Neoclassical ballet is the style of 20th-century classical ballet exemplified by the works of George Balanchine. The term "neoclassical ballet" appears in the 1920s with Sergei Diaghilev's Ballets Russes, in response to the excesses of romanticism and modernity.[29] It draws on the advanced technique of 19th-century Russian Imperial dance, but strips it of its detailed narrative and heavy theatrical setting. What is left is the dance itself, sophisticated but sleekly modern, retaining the pointe shoe aesthetic, but eschewing the well-upholstered drama and mime of the full-length story ballet.[30]Wikipedia:Verifiability

History and development

Neoclassical ballet is a genre of dance that emerged in the 1920s and evolved throughout the Twentieth Century. Artists of many disciplines in the early 1900s began to rebel against the overly dramatized style of the Romantic Period. As a result, art returned to a more simplistic style reminiscent of the Classical Period, except bolder, more assertive and free of distractions. This artistic trend came to be known as Neoclassicism. The ballet choreographer who most exemplified this new, clean aesthetic, was George Balanchine. As a child, the importance of classicism was imprinted on him when he was a student at the famed Imperial Ballet School, which was (and remains) steadfast in its firm commitment to classical ballet technique. Upon his graduation, Balanchine earned the privilege of choreographing for the Ballets Russes, where he had the opportunity to collaborate with Picasso, Matisse, Chanel, Debussy, Stravinsky and Prokofiev, who were all at the forefront of Neoclassicism. Rather than turning away from his classical training, Balanchine built upon the traditional ballet vocabulary. He extended traditional ballet positions, played with speed and freedom of movement, and incorporated new positions not traditionally seen in ballet. Balanchine's first foray into the neoclassical style was *Apollon Musegete*, choreographed in 1928 for the Ballets Russes, and set to a score by Stravinsky. Unlike many of his later neoclassical works, this ballet tells a story, which indicates that Balanchine had not yet completely broken free from the Romantic tradition. Moreover, when this ballet first premiered it featured large sets, costumes and props. However, Balanchine continually revised it as his neoclassical style evolved. For example, later versions of the ballet utilized white practice leotards and minimal sets and lights. Balanchine even renamed the ballet simply *Apollo*. The transformation of *Apollo* exemplifies Balanchine's transformation as a choreographer. As Balanchine's neoclassical style matured, he produced more plotless, musically driven ballets. Large sets and traditional tutus gave way to clean stages and plain leotards. This simplified external style allowed for the dancers' movement to become the main artistic medium, which is the hallmark of neoclassical ballet. https://www.youtube.com/watch?v=vZvyHxnu7DY

Balanchine found a home for his neoclassical style in the United States, when Lincoln Kirstein brought him to New York in 1933 to start a ballet company. He famously decided to start a school, where he could train dancers in the style he wanted, and so the School of American Ballet was founded in 1934. Many of his most famous neoclassical ballets were choreographed in the United States, on both his school eventually his own company, the New York City Ballet, which he founded in 1948 and still exists today. Well-known neoclassical ballets like *Concerto Barocco*, (1941), *Four Temperaments*, (1946), *Agon*, (1957), and *Episodes*, (1959) were all choreographed in New York.

Significant choreographers and works

Part of a series on
Classicism
Classical antiquity
• Greco-Roman world
Age of Enlightenment
• Neoclassicism • Economics • Music • Physics
20th-century neoclassicism
• Between World War I and II • Ballet • Economics • Music • Philosophy

- $\underline{v}$
- $\underline{t}$
- $\underline{e}^{31}$

Although much of Balanchine's work epitomized the genre, some choreographers like the British Frederick Ashton and Kenneth MacMillan were also great neoclassical choreographers.Wikipedia:Citation needed

- George Balanchine
  - *Apollo* (1928)
  - *The Prodigal Son* (1929)
  - *Serenade* (1934)
  - *Concerto Barocco* (1941)
  - *Symphony in C* (1947)
  - *Agon* (1957)
  - *Jewels* (1967)
- Serge Lifar
  - *Les Créatures de Prométhée* (1929)
  - *Le Spectre de la rose* (personal version) (1931)
  - *L'Après-midi d'un faune* (personal version) (1935)
  - *Icare* (1935)
  - *Istar* (1941)
  - *Suite en Blanc* (1943)
- Frederick Ashton
  - *Symphonic Variations* (1946)
  - *Cinderella* (1948)
  - *Sylvia* (1952)
  - *Romeo and Juliet* (1956)
  - *Ondine* (1958)
  - *La Fille Mal Gardee* (1960)
  - *The Dream* (1964)
- Roland Petit
  - *Le jeune homme et la mort* (1946)
  - *Carmen* (1949)
  - *Notre-Dame de Paris* (1965)
  - *Proust, ou Les intermittences du coeur* (1974)
  - *Clavigo* (1999)
- Kenneth MacMillan
  - *Romeo and Juliet* (1965)
  - *Anastasia* (1967)
  - *L'histoire de Manon* (1974)
- Jerome Robbins
  - *Dances at a Gathering* (1969)

- John Cranko
  - *Onegin* (1965)
  - *The Taming of the Shrew* (1969)

Contemporary ballet

Contemporary ballet is a genre of dance that incorporates elements of classical ballet and modern dance. It employs classical ballet technique and in many cases classical pointe technique as well, but allows greater range of movement of the upper body and is not constrained to the rigorously defined body lines and forms found in traditional, classical ballet. Many of its attributes come from the ideas and innovations of 20th-century modern dance, including floor work and turn-in of the legs.

History

George Balanchine is often considered to have been the first pioneer of contemporary ballet. However, the true origin of contemporary ballet is credited to Russian art producer Serge Diaghilev. Diaghilev wanted to bring an understanding of the arts to the general public. He created a program that combined all forms of the arts (painting, music, theater, and art) to present to the public. When this program had success in Russia, Diaghilev was inspired to bring it to a European audience by creating a new spin on classical ballet. He created Diaghilev's Russian Ballet Company, debuting the first show in 1909. However, Diaghilev was not a choreographer, he entrusted the evolvement of his creation to several well-known choreographers, one of them being George Balanchine. The style of dance Balanchine developed, which lies between classical ballet and today's contemporary ballet, is known by today's standards as neoclassical ballet. He used flexed hands (and occasionally feet), turned-in legs, off-centered positions and non-traditional costumes, such as leotards, tunics and "powder puff" tutus instead of "pancake" tutus, to distance his work from the classical and romantic ballet traditions. Balanchine invited modern dance performers such as Paul Taylor in to dance with his company, the New York City Ballet, and he worked with modern dance choreographer Martha Graham, which expanded his exposure to modern techniques and ideas. During this period, other choreographers such as John Butler and Glen Tetley began to consciously combine ballet and modern techniques in experimentation.

Figure 33: *A contemporary ballet leap*

Figure 34: *A contemporary ballet dancer*

Figure 35: *George Balanchine, a contemporary ballet pioneer*

Choreographers

One dancer who trained with Balanchine and absorbed much of this neoclassical style was Mikhail Baryshnikov. Following Baryshnikov's appointment as artistic director of the American Ballet Theatre in 1980, he worked with various modern choreographers, most notably Twyla Tharp. Tharp choreographed *Push Comes To Shove* for ABT and Baryshnikov in 1976; in 1986 she created *In The Upper Room* for her own company. Both of these pieces were considered innovative for their use of distinctly modern movements melded with the use of pointe shoes and classically trained dancers—for their use of contemporary ballet.

Tharp also worked with The Joffrey Ballet, founded in 1957 by Robert Joffrey. She choreographed *Deuce Coupe* for them in 1973, using pop music and a blend of modern and ballet techniques. The Joffrey Ballet continued to perform numerous contemporary pieces, many choreographed by co-founder Gerald Arpino.

Other notable contemporary choreographers include Jorma Elo, William Forsythe (choreographer), Mark Morris (choreographer), Jiri Kylian, Alonzo King, and Trey McIntyre.

Technique

Contemporary ballet draws from both modern dance and classical ballet for its training methods and technique. For a dancer to be able to embody various styles the training regimen has become more diverse. In addition to classical technique, which often includes the signature speed and style of George Balanchine for American dancers, dancers study modern as well. In addition, many dancers do various forms of cross training. Pilates and yoga are often included to loosen muscles and align the body. Since the late 1920s, Pilates has been a popular form of cross training to help prevent injury, but increasingly, the Gyrotonic Expansion System is being utilized. With contemporary work, dancers' spines need to be more supple and they need to understand how to be grounded. This is in contrast to classical and neoclassical ballet where the dancers are required to "pull up" and the upper body is held. Dancers are required to first obtain classical ballet training in order to build on it with more modern technique in order to be more versatile. Despite formal training, dancers are often affected by ankle injuries, due to the high intensity footwork.

Costumes

The costumes and footwear differ from any other style of dance as well. In contemporary ballet, dancers can be asked to wear pointe shoes, regular ballet shoes, or even no shoes at all. The same versatile approach goes for the music, setting, and costumes. Contemporary ballet does not require certain standards to be met. While it has more guidelines that modern dance, it does not conform to the limits of classical ballet. Classical ballet requires tutus, pointe shoes and scenery. Contemporary ballet uses different types of costumes, ranging from traditional to more modern tunic type versions. The music choices may vary as well. In Classical ballet, most often the choreography is done to classical music. In contemporary ballet, the music can range from the traditional classical music to popular music of today.

Present Day

Today there are many contemporary ballet companies and choreographers all over the world. Notable companies include Nederlands Dans Theater, Hubbard Street Dance Chicago, Complexions Contemporary Ballet, and Alonzo King LINES Ballet. Likewise, many traditionally "classical" companies also regularly perform contemporary works. Most classically trained dancers who may identify as professional ballet dancers are in fact required to be very versatile and able to perform work ranging from classical to neoclassical to contemporary ballet to modern dance. They are required to have impeccable ballet technique with a mastery of pointe technique for women, but at the same time, are being asked to be just as comfortable in ballet slippers or bare foot performing the work of modern choreographers such as Paul Taylor (choreographer) or embracing Gaga (dance vocabulary) in the work of Ohad Naharin. It is very common for ballet companies to have an official choreographer in residence to create new work—often contemporary—on the company. As well, many contemporary choreographers are commissioned to go to companies to create new work or a company will pay for the rights to perform already existing work and an official repetiteur will come to stage it. Twyla Tharp, as previously mentioned, is a highly renowned choreographer whose work is widely performed.

Appendix

References

[1] National Ballet Academy & Trust of India http://delhiballet.blogspot.com.au/2009/03/national-ballet-academy-trust-of-india.html?m=1 in New Delhi, India. Retrieved March 29, 2010.

[2] Chantrell (2002), p. 42.

[3] Kirstein (1952), p. 4.

[4] Thoinot Arbeau, _Orchesography_, trans. by Mary Steware Evans, with notes by Julia Sutton (New York: Dover, 1967)

[5] Lee (2002), p. 29.

[6] «Catherine de' Medici (1519-1589)» http://michaelminn.net/andros/biographies/de_medici_catherine, article from September 1990, published on "Andros on Ballet" page, on Michael Minn website.

[7] Vuillier, Gaston (1898). of Dancing from the Earliest Ages to Our Own Times https://books.google.com/books?id=xNnZzTJTWLEC&lpg=PP1&pg=PA65#v=onepage&q=&f=false' 'History, pp. 65–69. New York: D. Anderson and Company. [Facsimile reprint (2004): Whitefish, Montana: Kessinger Publishing.]

[8] Bland (1976), p. 43.

[9] Frances A. Yates, _The French Academies of the Sixteenth Century_, 2nd ed. (London: Routledge, 1988)

[10] Anderson (1992), p. 32.

[11] Cooper, Elizabeth (2004). "Le Balet Comique de la Reine, 1581: An Analysis" http://depts.washington.edu/uwdance/dance344reading/bctextp1.htm. University of Washington website.

[12] Lee (2002), p. 54.

[13] Bland (1976), p. 49.

[14] Costonis, Maureen Needham (1992). "Beauchamps [Beauchamp] Pierre" in Sadie (1992) 1: 364.

[15] Rosow, Lois (1992). "Lully" in Sadie (1992) 3: 82–89.

[16] Lee (2002), pp. 72–73.

[17] Lee (2002)., p. 73.

[18] Lee (2002), p. 74. Anderson (1992), p. 42.

[19] Pitt, Charles (1992). "Paris" in Sadie (1992) 3: 856.

[20] Kassing, Gayle. History of dance : an interactive arts approach. Champaign, IL: Human Kinetics, 2007. Print.

[21] Музыкальная энциклопедия. Гл. ред. Ю. В. Келдыш. Т 1. А — Гонг. 1072 стб. с илл. М.: Советская энциклопедия, 1973

[22] Чингиз Абдуллаев: «Вместо того, чтобы отталкивать нас, россиянам надо менять свои взгляды и отношение к народам бывших союзных республик» http://www.analytique.md/index.php?n=725&r=21&s=737
...первый балет на мусульманском востоке появился у нас.

[23] Большая Советская Энциклопедия. Гл. ред. А. М. Прохоров, 3-е изд. Т. 1. А — Ангоб. 1969. 608 стр., илл.; 47 л. илл. и карт, 1 отд. л. табл.

[24] George Balanchine

[25] https://www.jstor.org/stable/3020187

[26] https://books.google.com/books?hl=en&lr=&id=nx_0AAAAMAAJ&oi=fnd&pg=PA1&dq=Russian+Ballet+&ots=4LCkYWXxEo&sig=cOoulzxJIcmalFY2QxOVIdE9N3g

[27] https://web.archive.org/web/20080405224036/http://www.national.ballet.ca/pdf/education/Beginners%20Guide%20to%20Ballet.pdf

[28] http://www.national.ballet.ca/pdf/education/Beginners%20Guide%20to%20Ballet.pdf

[29] Serge Diaghilev: Ballet Impressario http://myballetsrusses.blogspot.ch/2011/08/serge-diaghilev-ballet-impressario-died.html

[30] http://www.washingtonballet.org/news-media/ballet-101/

[31] //en.wikipedia.org/w/index.php?title=Template:Classicism&action=edit

Article Sources and Contributors

The sources listed for each article provide more detailed licensing information including the copyright status, the copyright owner, and the license conditions.

Ballet *Source:* https://en.wikipedia.org/w/index.php?oldid=865539984 *License:* Creative Commons Attribution-Share Alike 3.0 *Contributors:* *Treker, .45Colt, 23smitlk, AH997, AJim, Adam9007, Ajiwon061, Albaballet, Amal-Tallal, Amys eye, Antique Rose, Apap04, Aquegg, Asilchenko, Asklf, Athenadancedaughter, Athomeinkobe, BU Rob13, Bazonka, BilCat, Bojo1498, Bruce1ee, CLCStudent, Cannolis, Chless, CiPokemonDancer, CityOfSilver, ClueBot NG, Colonel Wilhelm Klink, Cote d'Azur, D4R1U5, DRAGON BOOSTER, Dalliance, Dannyquan123, Davey2010, David Hightower, David in DC, David.moreno72, Daviermaia, Dcirovic, Deli nk, Diana fara, DocWatson42, Donner60, Dubs145, Ejmiles, Emmaannbange, Excirial, Favonian, Frosty, Gap9551, Gilliam, Goose Bolton, Graham87, Guanaco, Hairhorn, HanotLo, Howkafkaesque, Hiimy67, I AM Ajaneeta, I dream of horses, IJBall, IVORK, IdreamofJeanie, Insertcleverphrasehere, Iridescent, Jackfork, Jaguar, JamesLucas, Jaminstiefel122303, Jerome Kohl, Jessica18855667788, Jfoley1211, Jim1138, Jschnur, Just a guy from the KP, KAP03, KH-1, Katie12345678, Keith D, KiL92, Kleuske, KrisEd2009, KylieTastic, L3X1, LakesideMiners, Lambtron, LearnMore, Lhsa Love, Liance, Logger in denial, Logicalgenius3, LouisianaEdits, LuLu5!, Lucas.me, LuigiPortaro29, MAHOY, MB, Macedonian, Marisawriter, Matt294069, Mcmatter, Meamemg, MelbourneStar, Mlle Diana, Mr. Guye, Narky Blert, Nataliepalermo, NeilN, Nikkimaria, Nikolaiho, Norwikian, Oshwah, Paaaris, Paul foord, Person person with extra person on top, PetarM, PhoenixLumen, Qaei, Random86, Rchard2scout, Redneckballerina50, Ringoballerina, RunnyAmiga, Rwessel, SGOtter, Sandgem Addict, Sarahj2107, Sarahseller, Sattakishadow Basu, Sct72, SemiHypercube, Ser Amantio di Nicolao, Serois, Shahrux, Shellwood, Skm0321, Solomon7968, Spliterina, Stellastars132, StevenJ81, SuperTurboChampionshipEdition, Susbro, Sydney the cookie, Symphony in C, ThePlatypusofDoom, Tobybradford, Treefroglover777, Tripofmice, Truthful one, TwoTwoHello, WQUlrich, Weegaweek, Weirdoquerty, WereSpielChequers, West.andrew.g, Wfm123, Wikieditor8812, Wikipelli, Willthacheerleader18, Wolfpup98, Wtmitchell, Zefr, Zingarese, ZorbaDGeek, 161 anonymous edits 1

Timeline of ballet *Source:* https://en.wikipedia.org/w/index.php?oldid=776317292 *License:* Creative Commons Attribution-Share Alike 3.0 *Contributors:* Chicken10101, Chris the speller, Cote d'Azur, Gamewizard71, Hmains, Hooperbloob, Insouciance, Ipigott, JeffW, Johnbod, LiniShu, Nrswanson, Ohka-, Onionmon, Paul foord, Robertgreer, Will.i.am, Yamara, 4 anonymous edits 19

History of ballet *Source:* https://en.wikipedia.org/w/index.php?oldid=860257612 *License:* Creative Commons Attribution-Share Alike 3.0 *Contributors:* Alexius08, Allanth, Andrew Parodi, Anon685, BD2412, Balletfanindia, Bassonista, Bebokkos, Blurpeace, Bobby113133, Bsadowski1, CAPTAIN RAJU, Caviarmilk, Cdn14, Chris the speller, ClueBot NG, Cote d'Azur, D6, DASHBotAV, Darkwind, Dcirovic, De la Marck, Delusion23, Demeter~enwiki, Dkreisst, Docu, Donner60, Dricherby, E.Zajdel, Eliezg, Emotional Wiki Dude, Excirial, Flappychappy, Fleur-de-farine, Flyer22 Reborn, Fram, FunkyCanute, Gabyalaila, Gbern3, Gilliam, Gjescobedo, Grubby Snubby, HalfShadow, Hayman30, Hmains, Hqb, Ipigott, Jason Quinn, Jim10701, Jim1138, JimVC3, John of Reading, Khazar2, Kodama myszata, Kristen Eriksen, Kuru, L1A1 FAL, Lambtron, LilHelpa, Liz, Llightex, MKoala, MRD2014, Mordkin, Mriopez2681, My name is not dave, NastalgicCam, Non-dropframe, Nrswanson, Omnipaedista, Oshwah, OttawaAC, Paul foord, Pinethicket, Prad Nelluru, PunkBallet, Rising*From*Ashes, Rjensen, Robert.Allen, Robertgreer, Rosarino, Sacto4525, Sangre5, Serols, Shahrux, Sheffield3113, Stealthound, Takeaway, Tassedethe, TechLight, The Sage of Stamford, TheQ Editor, Tony1, Trey314159, Upabnela1986, VeryGoodsource1234, Vidshow, Wavelength, Wayne Slam, Widr, William Avery, William2001, Willthacheerleader18, Woohookitty, Yamaguchi先生, Zaslav, 166 anonymous edits 20

Classical ballet *Source:* https://en.wikipedia.org/w/index.php?oldid=842439658 *License:* Creative Commons Attribution-Share Alike 3.0 *Contributors:* Abberley2, Ahoerstemeier, Altenmann, Ani stefanovska, Antandrus, BU Rob13, Bobianite, CerealBabyMilk, Cjhamh, Ckatz, ClueBot NG, Commons-Delinker, Cote d'Azur, Crazy-dancing, DANE YOUSSEF, DavidLeighEllis, Ddrxn, Debresser, Ellywa, EoGuy, Epbr123, Erianna, Euchiasmus, Failmaster11, Fairgoldberry, Flowanda, GLG GLG, Gilliam, Graymornings, Helpsome, Herbertxu, HexaChord, Hubblebubble999, Ikindaknowaboutballet, Ipigott, Jason Quinn, Jennifu, John254, Jóna Þórunn, Kappa, Katrinity391, Keartime, Keitei, Khazar2, Killing Vector, Kiwiberries, Lambtron, LarRan, Lifefeed, Loadmaster, MPerel, Marsman8, Meatsgains, MikeyTMNT, Mild Bill Hiccup, Mimihitam, Mriopez2681, NaminesPetals, Nathan, Niteowlneils, Non-dropframe, Olsonist, Paul foord, Phmerz, Pion, Prolog, Reedy, Rjwilmsi, Robertgreer, Sanfranman59, Saturn star, Sedonaarizona, Slhogan94, Stoshmaster, Subitosera, Tassedethe, The Thing That Should Not Be, The cattr, Trevor MacInnis, Vacation9, VoABot II, Widr, Will.i.am, Yodada69, Yolobeomodksks, Yomama123. 6969696, Yurrmuma68, ZorbaDGeek, شكر زي, 127 anonymous edits 39

Romantic ballet *Source:* https://en.wikipedia.org/w/index.php?oldid=860516845 *License:* Creative Commons Attribution-Share Alike 3.0 *Contributors:* AxelBoldt, Ballongguy, Butterflybubbah, CBurns1101, Cholmes75, ClueBot NG, Cote d'Azur, Dbenbenn, Ekuns, Fbarton, Flauto Dolce, Frietjes, Gurch, Heimstern, Hemlock Martinis, Iron Pearl, Jack1956, Jessicapierce, Kasyapa, Kevin Ryde, KnightRider~enwiki, LittleWink, LouisAlain, Louise Dennis, Lyellin, Marysays, MicaHope, Michael Devore, Mrlopez2681, Nlu, Nv8200pa, Nzd, Ohka-, Onjacktallcuca, PBS-AWB, Robert.Allen, Robertgreer, Ross Uber, Sam Hocevar, Sophysduckling, SpiritedMichelle, Taglioni123, 88 anonymous edits 45

Neoclassical ballet *Source:* https://en.wikipedia.org/w/index.php?oldid=807595045 *License:* Creative Commons Attribution-Share Alike 3.0 *Contributors:* Andreasmperu, Bernstein2291, Cg2p0B0u8m, Chris the speller, Cote d'Azur, Dasani, DocWatson42, Frietjes, Jerome Kohl, John of Reading, Keitei, Kpjas, Lyellin, Marysays, Miagirljmw14, Mimihitam, Ohka-, OttawaAC, Paul foord, Phuzion, PrimateMover, Radagast83, Robertgreer, SaintAloysius, Slhogan94, SophieElisabeth, Sparafucil, Stevouk, TYelliot, TimNelson, 37 anonymous edits 50

Contemporary ballet *Source:* https://en.wikipedia.org/w/index.php?oldid=865038496 *License:* Creative Commons Attribution-Share Alike 3.0 *Contributors:* A.Minkowski, Adacore, Aliceko1, Andreasmperu, Anna Frodesiak, Annalisegardner, AnnieDTSF2002, Becchinamia, Biglovinb, Chris the speller, Citizen Canine, Ckatz, ClueBot NG, Cote d'Azur, DASHBotAV, DancingPhilosopher, David Shankbone, Delusion23, Dkreisst, Eemem, Ekahhisheek, Epanchin, Epbr123, FourViolas, Frietjes, Greman Knight, Gurchzilla, Howkafkaesque, I believe in the arts, Igoldste, Jackmcbarn, KH-1, KagamiNoMiko, Keitei, Kivary, Kiwiberries, Lambtron, Lmcburnett, LouisianaEdits, Mais oui!, Mb343, Mellis76, Mimihitam, Myznt, Paul foord, Radagast83, Rich Farmbrough, Robertgreer, Roland2~enwiki, Samuronin, Slhogan94, Spencer, THDju, Tassedethe, Tessbarnet, Trey McIntyre Project, Yamaguchi先生, Zadcat, 67 anonymous edits 53

Image Sources, Licenses and Contributors

The sources listed for each image provide more detailed licensing information including the copyright status, the copyright owner, and the license conditions.

Image *Source:* https://en.wikipedia.org/w/index.php?title=File:Padlock-silver-light.svg *Contributors:* User:AzaToth, User:Eleassar 1
Figure 1 *Source:* https://en.wikipedia.org/w/index.php?title=File:Degas-_La_classe_de_danse_1874.jpg *Contributors:* Alexandrin, Deadstar, Ecummenic, Fulvio314, Fæ, Infrogmation, Jan Arkesteijn, Jarekt, Judithcomm, Leyo, Makthorpe, Multichill, Pimbrils, Rlbberlin, Shakko, Siebrand, Skipjack, TwoWings, Un1c0s bot∼commonswiki, 1 anonymous edits 2
Figure 2 *Source:* https://en.wikipedia.org/w/index.php?title=File:Ballet_de_la_nuit_1653.jpg *Contributors:* Aiko, Bohème, Editor at Large, Huster, Jed, Judithcomm, MGA73bot2, Mattes, Mindmatrix, Qui1che, Shakko, Urdangaray, Warburg, Zhuyifei1999, 1 anonymous edits 3
Figure 3 *Source:* https://en.wikipedia.org/w/index.php?title=File:MarieSalle.jpg *License:* Public Domain *Contributors:* Ecummenic, Hsarrazin, Judithcomm, Kilom691, Leyo, Mu, William C. Minor, Wmpearl 4
Figure 4 *Source:* https://en.wikipedia.org/w/index.php?title=File:Swanlake015.jpg *License:* Creative Commons Attribution 2.0 *Contributors:* Paata Vardanashvili from Tbilisi, Georgia 5
Figure 5 *Source:* https://en.wikipedia.org/w/index.php?title=File:Giselle_-_Carlotta_Grisi_-_1841_-2.jpg *License:* Public Domain *Contributors:* Fleur-de-farine, Kilom691, Mrug, Mu, OgreBot 2 6
Figure 6 *Source:* https://en.wikipedia.org/w/index.php?title=File:Grace_in_winter,_contemporary_ballet.jpg *License:* Creative Commons Attribution-Sharealike 2.0 *Contributors:* jeff from denver, US 7
Image *Source:* https://en.wikipedia.org/w/index.php?title=File:Flower_Festival_01.jpg *License:* Public Domain *Contributors:* BotMultichill, Hilohello, Judithcomm, Lambtron, LittleTiny, PanteraRosa 8
Figure 7 *Source:* https://en.wikipedia.org/w/index.php?title=File:Agrippina_Vaganova_-_Esmeralda_1910.jpg *License:* Public Domain *Contributors:* Unknown [] 9
Figure 8 *Source:* https://en.wikipedia.org/w/index.php?title=File:Cecchetti_jpg.gif *License:* Public Domain *Contributors:* Castañor, Fleur-de-farine, Judithcomm, Tbonny, ͱ ͱ 10
Figure 9 *Source:* https://en.wikipedia.org/w/index.php?title=File:August_Bournonville_by_E._Lange.jpg *License:* Public Domain *Contributors:* E. Lange 11
Figure 10 *Source:* https://en.wikipedia.org *Contributors:* FlickreviewR 2, Fæ 12
Figure 11 *Source:* https://en.wikipedia.org/w/index.php?title=File:Suzanne_Farrell_and_George_Balanchine_NYWTS.jpg *License:* Public Domain *Contributors:* Orlando Fernandez, World Telegram staff photographer 13
Figure 12 *Source:* https://en.wikipedia.org/w/index.php?title=File:Anna_Pavlova_1912.jpg *License:* Public Domain *Contributors:* Bogomolov.PL, Fleur-de-farine, GMLSX, Infrogmation, PanteraRosa, The Deceiver, Torvindus∼commonswiki, ͱ ͱ ͱ 14
Figure 13 *Source:* https://en.wikipedia.org *Contributors:* Fleur-de-farine, Mari-lance, OgreBot 2 15
Image *Source:* https://en.wikipedia.org/w/index.php?title=File:Commons-logo.svg *Contributors:* logo *Contributors:* Anomie, Callanecc, CambridgeBayWeather, Jo-Jo Eumerus, RHaworth 16
Image *Source:* https://en.wikipedia.org/w/index.php?title=File:Wiktionary-logo-en-v2.svg *Contributors:* User:Dan Polansky, User:Smurrayinchester 17
Image *Source:* https://en.wikipedia.org/w/index.php?title=File:Wikisource-logo.svg *License:* Creative Commons Attribution-Sharealike 3.0 *Contributors:* ChrisiPK, Guillom, INeverCry, Jarekt, JuTa, Leyo, Lokal Profil, MichaelMaggs, NielsF, Rei-artur, Rocket000, Romaine, Steinsplitter 17
Figure 14 *Source:* https://en.wikipedia.org/w/index.php?title=File:Ballet_1582.png *License:* Public Domain *Contributors:* Alonso de Mendoza, Bohème, Conscious, Electron, G.dallorto, Judithcomm, Kocio, Man vyi, Martiny, Mu, Paris 16, Robert.Allen, Vincent Steenberg, Wst, 3 anonymous edits 20
Figure 15 *Source:* https://en.wikipedia.org/w/index.php?title=File:Sleeping_beauty_cast.jpg *License:* Public Domain *Contributors:* User:Barrie 21
Figure 16 *Source:* https://en.wikipedia.org/w/index.php?title=File:Ballet_1582.png *License:* Public Domain *Contributors:* Alonso de Mendoza, Bohème, Conscious, Electron, G.dallorto, Judithcomm, Kocio, Man vyi, Martiny, Mu, Paris 16, Robert.Allen, Vincent Steenberg, Wst, 3 anonymous edits 22
Figure 17 *Source:* https://en.wikipedia.org/w/index.php?title=File:Ballet_de_la_nuit_1653.jpg *Contributors:* Aiko, Bohème, Editor at Large, Huster, Jed, Judithcomm, MGA73bot2, Mattes, Mindmatrix, Qui1che, Shakko, Urdangaray, Warburg, Zhuyifei1999, 1 anonymous edits 24
Figure 18 *Source:* https://en.wikipedia.org/w/index.php?title=File:Daniel_Rabel_-_The_Royal_Ballet_of_the_Dowager_of_Bilbao's_Grand_Ball_-_WGA18593.jpg *License:* Public Domain *Contributors:* Hsarrazin, Jed, Judithcomm, Léna 25
Figure 19 *Source:* https://en.wikipedia.org/w/index.php?title=File:Ballet_Carneval_von_Venedig_Berlin_1827.jpg *License:* Public Domain *Contributors:* Kirchhoff 27
Figure 20 *Source:* https://en.wikipedia.org/w/index.php?title=File:Marie-taglioni-in-zephire.jpg *License:* Public Domain *Contributors:* Albertomos, AndreasPraefcke, Deadstar, Editor at Large, Ephraim33, Fleur-de-farine, Infrogmation, Jbarta, Lambtron, Laura1822, Mattes, Michael Bednarek, Opponent, Tbonny, Un1c0s bot∼commonswiki 28
Figure 21 *Source:* https://en.wikipedia.org/w/index.php?title=File:Swanlakemordkin.jpg *License:* Public Domain *Contributors:* Calliopejen, Fleur-de-farine, Infrogmation, Judithcomm, Kaganer, Mari-lance, Mariluna, Tbonny, 1 anonymous edits 29
Figure 22 *Source:* https://en.wikipedia.org/w/index.php?title=File:Pavlova_Anna_as_a_bacchante_in_The_Seasons.jpg *License:* Public Domain *Contributors:* Unknown photographer. [Original uploader was Mrlopez2681 at en.wikipedia] 31
Figure 23 *Source:* https://en.wikipedia.org/w/index.php?title=File:Vaslav_Nijinsky_in_Le_spectre_de_la_rose_1911_Royal_Opera_House.jpg *License:* Public Domain *Contributors:* Robert.Allen, Shakko 32
Figure 24 *Source:* https://en.wikipedia.org/w/index.php?title=File:La_Mort_du_Cygne_1_Anna_Pavlova_2_Yvette_Chauvire_3_Natalia_Makarova.mpg.OGG *Contributors:* 33
Figure 25 *Source:* https://en.wikipedia.org/w/index.php?title=File:Ballets_Russes_-_Apollo_musagète.jpg *License:* Public Domain *Contributors:* BotMultichill, Dierker, Fleur-de-farine, Lambtron, Macdonald-Ross, O (bot), Tbonny, Thyra 35
Figure 26 *Source:* https://en.wikipedia.org/w/index.php?title=File:Allah_Garibou.jpg *License:* Creative Commons Attribution-Sharealike 3.0 *Contributors:* User:JBGS 35
Figure 27 *Source:* https://en.wikipedia.org/w/index.php?title=File:Edgar_Germain_Hilaire_Degas_005.jpg *License:* Public Domain *Contributors:* AndreasPraefcke, BotMultichill, Ecummenic, Emijrp, File Upload Bot (Eloquence), Fleur-de-farine, Judithcomm, Leyo, Mandarine, Rlbberlin, Shakko, 1 anonymous edits 40
Figure 28 *Source:* https://en.wikipedia.org/w/index.php?title=File:Marie-taglioni-in-zephire.jpg *License:* Public Domain *Contributors:* Albertomos, AndreasPraefcke, Deadstar, Editor at Large, Ephraim33, Fleur-de-farine, Infrogmation, Jbarta, Lambtron, Laura1822, Mattes, Michael Bednarek, Opponent, Tbonny, Un1c0s bot∼commonswiki 41
Figure 29 *Source:* https://en.wikipedia.org/w/index.php?title=File:Ballet-Ballerina-1853.jpg *License:* Creative Commons Attribution-Sharealike 3.0 *Contributors:* Loadmaster (David R. Tribble) 42
Image *Source:* https://en.wikipedia.org/w/index.php?title=File:CecchettiStageLayout.png *License:* Creative Commons Attribution-Sharealike 3.0 *Contributors:* User:Lambtron 44
Image *Source:* https://en.wikipedia.org/w/index.php?title=File:RadStageLayout.gif *License:* Creative Commons Attribution-Sharealike 3.0 *Contributors:* User:Lambtron 44
Image *Source:* https://en.wikipedia.org/w/index.php?title=File:VaganovaStageLayout.gif *License:* Creative Commons Attribution-Sharealike 3.0 *Contributors:* User:Lambtron 44
Figure 30 *Source:* https://en.wikipedia.org/w/index.php?title=File:Three_Grces_-_Charles_Challon.JPG *License:* Public Domain *Contributors:* Alfred Edward Chalon (1780-1860) 46
Figure 31 *Source:* https://en.wikipedia.org/w/index.php?title=File:Pas-de-Quatre.jpg *License:* Public Domain *Contributors:* AndreasPraefcke, Fleur-de-farine, G.dallorto, Hilohello, Huster, Judithcomm, Lambtron, Salvor, SkedO, Tbonny 47
Figure 32 *Source:* https://en.wikipedia.org/w/index.php?title=File:Наталья_Колосова_кадр_1.jpg *License:* Public Domain *Contributors:* Зимин Василий геннадиевич 48
Figure 33 *Source:* https://en.wikipedia.org/w/index.php?title=File:ContemporaryBalletLeap.jpg *License:* Public Domain *Contributors:* Lambtron 54
Figure 34 *Source:* https://en.wikipedia.org/w/index.php?title=File:Grace_in_winter,_contemporary_ballet.jpg *License:* Creative Commons Attribution-Sharealike 2.0 *Contributors:* jeff from denver, US 54
Figure 35 *Source:* https://en.wikipedia.org/w/index.php?title=File:G._Balanchine_(young).jpg *License:* Public Domain *Contributors:* Bogomolov.PL, Testino1, Túrelio 55

License

Index

www.ingramcontent.com/pod-product-compliance
Lightning Source LLC
Chambersburg PA
CBHW020037040426
42331CB00031B/860